PLACES YOU LEAVE

Also by James Byrne with Arc Publications

POETRY
Blood / Sugar (Arc, 2009)
White Coins (Arc, 2015)
The Caprices (Arc, 2019)

POETRY (AS EDITOR)
Bones Will Crow with ko-ko thett (Arc, 2012)
Atlantic Drift with Robert Sheppard (Arc, 2017)
I Am a Rohingya with Shehzar Doja (Arc, 2019)

James Byrne
PLACES YOU LEAVE

PUBLICATIONS
2022

Published by Arc Publications,
Nanholme Mill, Shaw Wood Road
Todmorden OL14 6DA, UK
www.arcpublications.co.uk

978 1 910345 82 5 (pbk)

Design by Tony Ward
Printed in Great Britain by
TJ Books, Padstow, Cornwall

Cover image:
Collage painting by James Byrne

Arc Publications UK and Ireland Series:
Series Editor: Tony Ward

For my brother, Robin (1973-2020)
agoraphobic, unable to travel

Walking alongside his shadow, he suddenly realised that
it was both of them who needed to cross the border.

Yousif Qasmiyeh

… a wound where the blood of history does not dry.

Gayatri Chakravorty Spivak

… to converse is to divert language from itself
by letting it differ and defer…

Maurice Blanchot

CONTENTS

COX'S BAZAR

'Protect Names & Faces, Yes?'

You plant the jackfruit's anonymous, nubbled face and wait in the boiling sand for something to happen.

A goat's eye flashes gold. A girl swings on the tubewell for a cup of water.

You plant peas to grow in the monsoon and put on your best shirt. Yellow for optimism.

What is missing about the blank page is denied. Decimated, you would like to cohere.

Inside an airless, windowless hut, you try to re-write Stevens: Ten Ways of Looking at a Passport. 'I have never seen a passport, how does it begin?'

Toothmarks in the linebreak. You want to put the art back into heart.

When your brother ran towards the Tatmadaw, crying 'Jayzu, Jayzu', you turned and ran. Jahaj of air. Jail, lock and key.

Without 'art', it's just 'he', meaning brother. Come here, brother, but he isn't listening.

Your mother bribes the army guard to write a letter, asks about the non-trial. Will the guard deliver? Hope's lottery. There is no policy on answering the letters or the law. The page a windbreak. To write is to petition.

The 'I' severs you in the photograph, so we repose. Someone else must always be next to you. You cannot work alone.

13

Cyclonic clangour of rain. Sword-water in the Naf. The helicopter pumps into Bangladeshi airspace and fires on anyone swimming away.

The poem bare as a pulse, a knife. Siblings in graves.

The poem bare as a knife, a pulse.

Your father remains stuck on the border. 'Genocide Zone'. Nobody is reporting from there, so nothing is said.

The child draws pictures of a burning house. Singing out of history in makeshift schools.

You plant and write. Plant and write. What else is there to do? Peas on your roof grow beside the ashfire. You knot back the twine and forecast clouds.

You write: 'blot out', 'jail of air' and the words mean the same in the morning. Myanmar waits for the incendiary. The Saudis send money for guns. When you 'like' the post about ARSA, your cousin gets a note under his hut.

'Ze zaga añra félai ay zaígoí'. 'There are places we leave' you say. 'There are places we never leave. Home is a dream inside a nightmare'.

The first line of your first poem begins: 'I am afraid of someone I don't know'.

Last night your mother peeled back the tarpaulin and asked: 'what are you doing, my son, why can you not sleep? Sleep!' And you replied: 'Emily Dickinson, Emily Dickinson'.

You ignore the honking of the UNHCR truck, check the download speed for '100 Poets in English' (to learn poetry, to learn English). Reload.

Already they are looking to blame the same someone. The Chinese highway needs to be paid.

Looking at you. Between Paan branches brittled by soil erosion.

Why is it you live in the middle of the largest refugee camp in the world and they're calling it 'a lost treasure', a 'forgotten' national park?

They ask you to plant trees to 'save the environment'. Yes, you think. A few more trees to hide the smell of the latrine.

How do you write about 'environment'? You try for the present, the sensory, but your eyes sting, your ears hum and the smell is flesh and smoke.

'I want to write about family, but I have no family.'

The idea of the eternal traveller does not hold. To think of poetry as orphic. To unthink memory: to unriver the severed head.

As if the world were a wound flapping its bandages.

As if the world were a wound. As if…

You wake up and poke your pen through the ash.

English ale. 'Dada eta ki gari?' High speed trains. This is where I am going.

An envelope stuffed with Taka. A bookmark. To hold nothing, to hold your place in the book.

DHAKA $\longrightarrow$ CHITTAGONG

'Life Raft Awaiting'

You stare into the night sky around Hatirjhil (Elephant Lake). Is it the heat that makes you sigh like this? Yes, it is the heat and my delusions of suffering.

A server pours cha. You sit on the porch and shake off the dust from your *Dhaka Club Chronicles*.

Tomorrow, from a penthouse balcony, in the middlenight clearing its throat and through alchemic clouds of shisha.

Tomorrow, tomorrow, wait for tomorrow.

In the morning – Ahsan Manzil's pinkness winking through palm trees – you meet Alimullah the social worker. What does it mean to the founder of Nawab Atikullah, to be known by the title 'sponsor of art and literary activities'?

The portrait replies, cold and public. Portrait of a portrait, aversion to a versioning.

You write your name on the land paper. First in Persian, then for the British. Deeds of land evidence futureshock. The soot of empire.

1905: Land deed from Fuller to the Governor of Bengal and Assam: 'to help this backward community'.

The eye struck blind by oblivion. Fuller, as in Sir Fooler on the banks of the Buriganga. But nobody is fooling.

Smedley signs for the Nawab [NO NAME]. Khwaja Adbul [WIFE UNKNOWN]. Khaya Parer Taram meets the queen, bows, shatters the family portrait.

During the liberation war, Sufia Kumal appeared at her window saying: 'I am not dead, I am not dead, I am not dead.'

A full moon disappears behind thick white clouds to wipe its face.

'She was a good horserider who even earned her good name by embracing men'. She who arises or falls, or is absent, as if missing (but not missing). Missed out.

She, the only feminist in the palace. She who worked with 'women's issues'. She, fighting off 'His Lordship's Leopard'. The longshot of logic.

You walk through your own whiteness: an open door.

Bamfyeld over billiards zones his eye on the Nawab's daughter skipping into the Ballroom. He breaks, scatters the balls, fouls, leaves with a huff of apology.

In the palace painting, all the daughters sit at the front. You follow them through the canvas, call them 'truly exotic in their beauty'. But the truth is plural and the exotic walks on air.

'From the windows of / this / room, I sit helpless, / waiting, / silent – sister'.

Between red-washed curtains, you stare through the girl's earlobes. Carnal ticking. Between the music, so much silence you can hear everything.

Bamfyeld will return in the Spring, without his Kentish bride. He is a young man of the world unravelling before him. A *great* man, a man of knowledge, of leisure and of the highest breeding.

The palace stultifies your breath.

Outside, air mollifies a skyline jagger of telephone lines. In the market, the pigeons are obediently tied to their cages. The chickens are wired. Wired up.

You climb through the fusshouse of centuries, looking for a Sadhu. His followers cram the aching darkness of hallways. They wait for him to return from lunch.

Starling scissors. Egret confetti wings. You see this, shut up inside four-walled luxury. You split the fish like protozoa.

And what will you ask when he returns? I will ask what food means to the soul of an empty body. If sleeping brings us any closer to reality. I will ask him to remove this invisible black mark from my forehead.

Windows look out on steeled cement. Fractioning of a sum. As if held by nothing and always falling, a stanchion raised to the broiling sun.

You fall away, street to river, day to dream. amphitheatre stage tends down towards the sleeping nurse-mother. Euripides among thorns, woken up, transformed into a mango tree. You wake up.

> To walk through the door   of your whiteness.

A mother sobs through cadmium, betel-stained teeth. Boys on either arm. And a third child – a daughter, younger and without legs – sits on a green muslin mat, wipes her mother's face.

Prayer's echolalia. Where are you from? Where do you go? Voice throwback to zero hour.

Safar, Sulami, Salaka. Tell me where and I will be going.

The footpath rips in both directions. The radio signals jam like traffic. The meeting place does not meet.

I want to meet you – I want to know what to do.

Old now tomorrow in the blackwater. Ganga to Ganges. The RAHMAN butcher sign's partitional rusts turns to jade. Reflection in The Eye Palace. Fracted and replicable.

Give me Allah's food to fill my stomach, she said.

As if it would be any clearer to you if only the dead were speaking. As if by deleting the face in the photograph, she might disappear and you would remember yourself.

Unlifed, living on. Speak now or forever speak of this.

When they stopped you at the checkpoint they put a gun to your head and asked you to beg Allah's forgiveness for being a refugee.

Mistranslation in the electoral banner: politicians would have you for blood.

THE WHOLE COUNTRY MOVES WITHIN US. But the traffic stalls an hour, held up by two bullocks. The deep wallop of their eyes.

In Gulshan, you surround yourself with books and work, work and books. Privilege-busy and in the seed-eat of thinking – so as not to think – you forget.

Shadow pass of an auntie making sabzi from a balcony window. Mother, wear the daughters face, scliffing bamboo from the tree. Koltar tek he.

You turn up the scripture page, echo the muezzin. 'Give charity from what God has given you… Should we feed the person whom God, if He wished, could feed?'

And so the question isn't a question, but what remains of wishing. Allah's food to fill my stomach. Will you meet me? I cannot meet you.

If the mother could wear the daughter's face. If anything can be wished, wish now.

        I want to meet you – I want to know what to do.

You wait on the balcony, cooling with lemonade. Such pleasure. Pleasuring decay.

Inside the cooking chambers of your house, meat cures in the sun. A chicken cut from the red net. Flute song of a lamb's marrow. A river's vein severs the sweating Delta.

It is as if you could ask for anything. A squareshare of land, a road, a garden for rain to drip through the rice. Not much to ask for, so you didn't.

Bismillah, he said. Split me into bricks and I will build a house.

MEXICO CITY $\longrightarrow$ PUEBLA $\longrightarrow$ MEXICO CITY

'Hermana in the web'

A muddy footprint fossilises on the WELCOME
mat at Puebla/Acapulco. ¡BIENVENIDOS! What
is thinking inside a steel suit, dangling fake jade?
The lie of friendship spread out like echeverría.
Cortés' tuele bones buried underneath the sensorial
gardens at Chapultepec. Breath's cortex toxifies
a chemicalised lago. Doña Marina whispers through
the deafness of Moctezuma's ear. What rings the skin
to marvel at a floating city for possession, trees
shaken into fire? Mala Madre. White snake dissects
the green leaves. Cortés, meaning courteous, polite.
Names, faces, washed out, as if clean in dirty water.

Standing on Tenochtitlán five hundred years ago,
what did you see, Bernal, beyond feathers, cloaks,
merchandise? *Male and female slaves to be sold
in the market.* White tower of history. Black holes.
The gaps between your teeth spell death. What
you understand to mean of money is multi-stranded,
like Paz's cyclical idea of conquest. No such thing as
making it, only taking it from the mouth of the world.
Polyconscious, as if you might fuse eyes by looking
into his eye. Mesoamerica FOXing your television,
Disneyfying the children. Pero cuando, pero
perdido. Bernal, what was it you saw on the road?

27

Face in the mirror's blade, muralised, Armstrong's
eyes blubber over the dials. As if anyone might control
the stars (Woodrow tried: first fix economic control,
he said, then you control another country's domestic
affairs). Garden vines shucked from the roots, rinsed
fire, democratic gasmasks. Workers protest at the vats.
You march through the bust of Socrates, count the days
to come in the lash marks on your back. ETERNIDAD
tattoos a skeleton's brow and Plutarco's head of teeth
smiling just for you. Canto of an open hand singing
from a fist. Eyes, ambient at the furnace, beauty's unfinishings.
Every movement moved for continuation.

Una Vida. Una Bala. One life. One bullet. You shoot
to pardon the executioner. To speak a single sentence
with a thousand bullets. To crack the colonial yoke.
To outflank skyscrapers and overthrow money. You
drink the cacao down, trade winds severed by Spanish
pesetas. Hipotecado. You re-mortgage. Just one cloud
to tarnish the day's panoramics. In the zócalo, in the halflight
of dawn, they form riot shields while the caballero
grips the butt of his gun. Shoot. Don't shoot. December,
1963, in the Plaza de Santo Domingo, your hands reach
through the departing train's wagon slats saying: no
jeres ir. Brown dust in your yellow shirt tight as skin.

Spit dries on Santa Ana at Tepeyac. Stone of Porfirio's
face on looking into his own grave in Père Lachaise. You
ride a boat to moor at your own death. Always believing
you might return, never to return. Overturned by la Bola
del Hante. Friendship for treason. 9th of February flips
inside your calendar, opens out on ten years of tragedy.
El Pueblo Cambio stained with blood. You looked into
the waterflow flowing west, so sure to be waiting it out,
for the revolution's bullets to end. But they didn't end.
Until now. Teenagers joust outside the monument in a rap
battle: 'tu hermana es bonita como tu madre / Tu madre
está cansada hoy'. Not facing you, the greater enemy.

What it means to pet the dog. Mornings outside the Jardín
Pushkin, they're selling dental pasta for Bowzer, selling
you out, leashed, with shitmutt plastic hands as scoopers.
Bowzer down, but no, he's pattering around the ancient
oaks, sniffing out piss tunnels, baking in the scratchyard.
Today is a family day. Children rustle poodles, a Scottie
crossbreed twizzles the testes of a Boxer for familiars.
To love you more than human. To shun the homeless man
tooting Greensleeves on a recorder. Unrecorded. During
conquest, the biggest killer of Mexicans was the Alaunt.
Rabbit in the mouth, just to get the smell of blood going.
To outstare Cuauhtémoc, his feet burning gold in the fire.

You dream of a tree lying down to become a road.
You dream of a road lying down to become a park.
Your wife sells Takis and solo cigarettes, agua filled
from the tap, sealed with a governmental blue seal.
A fattened Mini Mouse shadows her back on La Viga.
All the junk of useable colour strewn over Navifiesta,
Mugia's face in the underpass with the throat scratched
out. It is Tuesday and you're becoming forgetful since
there's always too much to remember. The Café Feliz,
closed, so you sit outside, unsheathing a smile towards
the face of your daughter. Dream of her taking a seat
at the Universidad Conversa. But she doesn't want to go.

At their centre, all cities lie, casting spells over the idea
of progress. Displace east, past the Agrícola Pantitlán.
The store on Zaragoza sells muscle pills. A life-size
doll of Conan's Schwarzenegger (or is it He-Man?)
stands proud on the pavement in imitation gold. No-one
else here, except for two girlfriends hugging into a smile
under the PEMEX pumps. Streets emptied by a volcano
of rain and gathering dusk. Oil prices rise. The centre
barely holds and the new government (say the oracles
of taxi drivers), merely one shade better than the last.
You turn the corner. A dog on Iztaccihuatl mounts
a taco tray, is hit sideways by the face of a guitar.

5646.4012. Nothing else on the billboard because
everyone knows what it means. The dialled number
doesn't connect, nobody's buying. Operation Escudo.
Operatif in the Cuidad Perdida. Spread your arms
like a plastic doll on Calle Lieja, flash past in the bus
at Nezahualcóyotl ('Neza'), the warriors' Sunday fast
snagged by roadblocks. Two boys hold up a plastic bag
on the dash, another kicks a football on a splattered
wall. You wonder at distances. Why it is the Wikipedia
links don't load the photos. At the border of Mexico
City and Puebla, two women clean the toilets, flick
bucket water before collapsing into laughter's heap.

You who would forgive the gran chingón, forgives
the tearing up of bridges. Who would build for him
a new bridge, enjoys the passive vitality of flowers
growing beside a washing line, or figs drying
on the harvest branch. Stranger to himself, unstrangered
by you, as if love were time meant to
extend nail coffins or call down from the cross your
fallen eagle. Material wounds of soil. Earth speaking
in your ear like Malinche in Siqueiros' 'Tormento'
(there's always a woman involved, right? Wrong).
Thunder echoes lightning, white lines streak against
the dark. You carry on existing, but forget to watch.

A moon in dialogue with a closing sun and the light
asking: what are they really doing down there? Bones
for eyes, Mictlantecuhtli, god of death, in your house
every day. So when death comes, you fear nothing, not
even the body's temple of sacrifice. On the bus radio
some show about the surviving speakers of Ayapa
who reunited from a feud to save their language.
Crosses divide the hills from the port, but the world
outside is silent. They sent priests with dialectical orders
from Veracruz, not to preserve, but to translate the mind
via torture or 'biblical conversion'. Pedro de Alvarado
swipes at idols, places a bloody cross over your mouth.

Lindo a Linda. Puebla's zocalo simmers in the sun.
A gardener snips trees with shears, turns, as he does,
to the most beautiful of young girls, misses the branch.
Root to shudder. It is Monday. The fiesta over. Children
walk back to school through cryptographical streets.
Calle decimosexto. Septiembre. Ache-weighty doors
to the cathedral and the Museo Bello y Zetina. At the
far end a white circle around the installation of an oak.
The plaque mentions a young girl flattened in the storm.
No name. Beneath the circle, students in tents camp out
under placards: LA VIOLENCIA SOBRE NOSOTROS ES UNA
FORMA DE CONTROL. Who was she? Who was she?

Everything grows, grows over. But the bougainvillea
persists, carrying its bright trauma. Wasp nest in the
archives of Von Humboldt, the 'scientific conquistador'.
Live in a house for long enough and you'll be haunted
you said. Buddleia fills the window frame on Oriente 5.
If you dig under the cathedral, you'll end up polishing
old bones. At the city limits, by a curling highway,
the Encore Hotel echoes axe-handle dust. A young boy
in the fields, seven or eight, stands at his fathers'
feet, tall as the corn leaves. His face, eager under
a hot bout of sun, to turn the blade, the soil, blood
to money, to become a man, or something like him.

From stoneshadow, your heart raises to The House
of the Sun and you are gone, in a shower of bladed
feathers. To forfeit the body, not to fight for its life.
Your heart is a gift, your blood carried as precious
water through a city. Tethered by fate as to the slab,
where you fight like a warrior with cudgels for arms.
You believe death is rehearsal, offered light, sacrifice
to the fifth sun. For the sky to inhale us like smoke,
bone-seed. Exchange for a captor's insignia, flowers,
tobacco pipes. You wake on the bus, from the vatic
snake of a dream. Who did you see last night? asks
your father. You tell him the lie of seeing nothing.

Sor Juana's child turned to bogeyman. You live
on the favella's quarry, but are new around here.
A Coca Cola truck filled with uncut base at Juárez,
you were caught, sent down to Puebla, keep quiet:
orders from the bosses, from the judge. You miss
the fish of Sinaloa, walk zócalo to park and back,
count the hours on a smashed clockface. A week
passes, hotel pimps hustled for change, you show
the girls your Alliance tattoo, form a construction
firm. Wet coke drying in cement bags, wet bodies
in body bags, the depot turned into a waste disposal.
Rings for antiquity. You cut the watches off yourself.

To sleep in the spiral of a rain basin's shadow. Blue
eye of Huitzilopochtli stares through his skull; city
subsoil, a sun erupts to calm the flood. You amplificate,
rock to hammer, things the Spanish loot to build museums.
Opening the armet's visor, he smiled, his face, *no araña
o cobra, lo Innominable*, but persistent as cactus leaves
growing from bare rock. To caw-caw inside the House
of Eagles, to split you into speechlessness. On Garibaldi,
the Americans cannot understand why you have to pay
for the serenade. The mariachi fixes a string with his teeth.
A hawker of scrap metal asks for your tortillas. You hand
over your plate, but the cook flaps him away with a towel.

Timeless Strength. Trotsky's cacti. Give strength.
A wishing well rouble lands tails. A stray thorn sickles
the leaf. Natalia dreams Frida's rose, and they expedite
in secret. Daytrips to Popocatépetl to watch a boy
packing horseshit, loggers on the backroads of Paso
Cortés. If you touch me I won't bleed he said, but did.
Rifles echo through the cocina, the dials of a transistor
scrambled, the Ediphone cut, a wooden typewriter
burned in the yard. You pick up Lenin's red handkerchief,
wipe your brow and wait for the silver bullet.
Morning, a tremble of rain and, now, this heft of sun.
A rooster in your garden gawks through the smoke.

On el al Jibes' I ♥ MEXICO graffiti wall, a girl,
maybe fifteen, poses in fishnets, push-up bra,
BABE hoodie. Her (boy)friend flashes the camera,
and another woman, disinterested, holds the silver
reflector. You watch, eating your tourist enchiladas,
Mystify Me playing over the speaker. She draws
a small crowd of teenage boys, who tut 'puta, puta'
at her, awkward. She smiles at them. Catalogue pose
fading as they pack up for the next block. You look
back at the wall. Bowie's 'Heroes for One Day',
speech-bubbling over the white eyes of the Reaper
dressed as Spiderman. 'Hermana' etched in the web.

35

Ojo de dios. Eye of the gods. Primary idol, it keeps
evil shut, swinging side-to-side on your dashboard
all through the city to the fixed beacon of the airport.
The huicholes believed the unseen becomes clearer,
but today, tomorrow, how would you know what clarity
looks like? Your face hazes in the mirror, an open mouth
clutching at thirst. As if Villaurrutia's ideas on love might
save you. Smile at the desert plain rolling past the distant
volcanoes. You step out the car, over-tip the driver, sensing
his embarrassment. At the departure gate, daughters, sons,
off to Houston, Dallas, or California. And you follow them,
through the clear glass of a gate, back your known limits.

Stiffneck at LAX. Border security. Still technically inside
Mexican territory (half a country of landmass taken away).
The frowny guard holds up your passport like a jeweller
working on a piece of filigree and asks, knowing full well,
why you were refused entry last year. 'Libya', you reply.
'Oh', he says, asking you to remove your glasses, checking,
with a squirrel's attentiveness the photograph, the ten-year
visa. 'I always wondered why that mad dictator had so much
money'. You are silent, thinking of his boss and the strange
simplicity of a nametag. 'Josh, you say, 'I wonder why half
the population of Mexico lives on less than a dollar a day.'
But it's too late. He avoids you now, stamped through.

QUITO $\rightarrow$ ESMERALDAS $\rightarrow$ QUITO

'Injustos'

Equatorial statue. You arrive at two figures meeting at the mouth of a gaping door. Close enough to be kissing. 'A metaphor for BREXIT', says Santi.

The buses spew toxic fume. A man dips his nose into a grey poncho. Cardinally, before his morning shift, the driver hands $100 to a police officer. Backslap the road towards upstairs rheostats.

Your coach is driven by two military officers. They wait for you, revving and unimpressed outside Miss Forever.

Inside the Iglesia de la Campania de Jesus, one of the angels carries the gold key of Easter. Choose from any of seven locked doors.

Black door of crucifixion. White door of silence.

In hell's mural, a king's head boils in an open vat. INJUSTOS written on his neck. Several cherubs breathe life into a dark cloud. A shelf of houses in Miravalle kiss the sky.

You head for the volcano-misted city of Machachi. The shitbasin now a museum of water. The mayor – keenly tanned, wristwatch machismo, hair as if pronged back – stands at the bridge applauding no-one in particular.

Over heaped ceviche, when you ask him for the time he replies: 'there is never any time'.

The mayor finishes his sentence by saying in a serious tone: 'La poesia es spiritualista'. He is not a man for loose discussion. Santi whispers to you why the mayor doesn't need to worry about re-election. He worships the populist con where all art is money.

The bright flowers in the garden are, you are told, the open eyes of poets. On a tomato-smeary napkin you write: the capitalist would extinguish poetry by ignoring it or – if anything might accrue – by buying it out.

When you read the referendum poem he folds his arms and whispers to his secretary, pulling her at the hip. Mayoral reports. Ministry of the hollow bargain.

At Cotopaxi, the censor records have been misplaced. Narcos billboards. Condor snare.

Face of the moon. Neck of the sun.

A black-eyed dog sleeps on the railway track. Bougainvillea severs the cross.

At night, a spider's chassis springs open from under the pillow of your Machachi patroness. A totem, nimble as blinking, scuttles into the white divan.

From heart-shaped ears sloping down to her neck, the patroness wears ivory opals. She is eager you sit with her, insisting on double portions for everyone. A felt glove touches your knee through the steak course. She orders a bell for the table (the kind no one uses in antique hotels) and places it beside the gloveless hand.

A guitarist plays while we eat and then eats alone. His wife sits opposite you and refuses to touch glasses. After playing 'Something in the Way', you ask his name and he says 'Jorge, after George Harrison'. His favourite four people in the world are John, Paul, George and Ringo, he says. His wife glances into the open hole of his mouth.

A young waiter flicks in from behind a curtain, palms glazed with rain. Driver, lover, waiter, he looks at you, apologetic, embarrassed and is dismissed, as if first by you.

'What shall I do today?' the patroness thinks. 'What is there ever to do?' the garden replies. Sun scalds latticed dew. The garden circuses all morning. A lithe cat paws a fly around the drained pond. A bird, russet grey, skims the ferns, lands on the honked-out statue of a goose.

Upstairs, a gallery of chaise longues, porcelain dolls, haberdashery, the secrecy of diaries. Ancestry's yowling mouth.

You burn like currency spent. Hover like a bookmark. Aslant, sensorial, quibbling as the weather of a Yes-No morning. From her chamber room, panpipes. A ram's head and a rifle hang from the door which does not open.

Back in the bus, a horse's tail brooms away the low cloud around Corazón. Cows, half chow at pasture or whip their tails towards the hills of Colón.

You traverse, highway to city, spraycanning: CORREA: TRAIDOR DE LA PUEBLO.

On the sideroad, a man selling doors. A woman peeling humitas. When he speaks to her it is like the loose turning of a hinge, the jimmying of a handle, a final slamming. She turns to her children, tears hardening into a smile. This is not how the story ends in the book.

Neck of the moon. Face of the sun.

White door of crucifixion. Black door of silence.

Tomorrow, my son would begin school, she says. But there is no money in school. He must learn how to see the world through this window.

Over a hotel's tinny speakers, Carmen Gonzalez sings 'Caramba'. Two teenagers wrestle beside a prostitute whose legs were seared for stealing a chicken.

Faded CHAMPIONS CHELSEA shirt, he squats behind the bars of his house at La Ranchera.

You must eat enough to become a man. You must move the world around your mouth as if tasting wine. You must sit on a burnt tyre swing and sing yourself into the future.

La razon yo / me pregunto / En donde esta la conciencia / la conciencia de esta mundo. Where is the reason / I question / Where is conscience / the conscience of the world?

In 'Simposio II', the shaman blows bubbles through a crowd. 'La Aparicion''s door is marked with a white crucifix.

Sol's firewheel. The earth, lecce marrón. The sewer a black lime. Your brother in the Basul tree, poised as a catapult.

You arrive into Esmeraldas. Emerald city. Afro-Ecuadorian, escaped slaves hiding from the Spanish. *Cimarrones.* Marooned, starved, raided.

The mayoress greets you from the bus. She is dressed in a snazzy eucalyptan suit, plants you a kiss and, on hearing you are British, decries:

> 'Mala política! El mundo es loco…'
> 'Sí, todo el mundo', you reply.

Rise to the logger's chainsaw smile. NO FLAMMABLE AQUI. Achillean thorn in the forest's heel. Memorial flowers – white and yellow – slatted in the valley's s-bend.

The abuela walks through cake mud in her flipflops. Corrugated panel thrown over a trembling puddle. Two children seesaw until stuck on a log's hierarchical point. Passion fruit in ash dust. Driftwood pyres on a plastic beach.

Accidentes meaning unevenness. Your eyes shake open. Like water drained along the equatorial line, one veers west, the other east.

At the reading, all the poets are men but for Margarita singing Lorca. You ask if she has a book and she hands you a CD with a postcard of the Pichincha saint waiting to be fitted with a head. White sky shot through her stomach.

'Quiero que entres en mis ojos y me ayudes a ver / el color de los anhelos que te hacen feliz.' I want you to enter my eyes, to help me see / the colour of yearning that makes you happy.

You take a front seat for the dance finale on the beach – disco sequins, purple and silver studded on black lycra – three male dancers hoist the lead girl up by the wrists, but Romeo does not catch her. Balcony sighs, she falls on her waist from twenty feet, is scooped up from the floor, groggy and elasticated.

In the curtain she checks for blood and picks you out in the audience as if to say: mi gancho, what have you done?

Nothing. I have done nothing.

A woman looks through you as she pisses behind a low wall of pineapples. Finned green iguana of the Pacific crashes over her shoulder.

The Bolivar statue in Plaza Santa Domingo points at you falling backwards, scattering the pigeons, as if to ask:

And what have you done in doing nothing?

A hill's pasture fogs into veined stone. Coughs up the traffic. Covers its mouth.

Nothing. I have done nothing.

You fall asleep in the zócalo and dream of a tiger wrapped around the neck of a lion. You wake to Garcia Moreno's hard stare and the sound of a man rinsing his teeth in the marble fountain.

Like Cantuña's devil at Francisco. Something in the world always missing or hidden.

You offer the boy your coffee but he refuses. 'Trabajo, mi trabajo'. You return with a sandwich and a ten dollar bill. He separates the meat, throws bread for the birds.

A man with stumps for arms rolls along the square on his spine. Arsecrack smiling sideways to the sun. 'Y para mi? y para mi?'

Nada me ha quedado de ese tiempo en que me amabas. Nothing has remained of the time in which you loved me.

A toddler in pink, cups a hand around a pigeon who flacks, shits itself in her hand.

You head for the house of La Mala Negra ('The Bad Black Woman') where the poets used to drink. Suits of Ecuadorian men on YouTube reimagine her in their image. In the video, there are no women. All the musicians are wearing ties.

On Morales, a tapestry without a face. The torn flag of the revolution gapes like a bruised eye.

Bullhead taxidermy for a maître'd. You take a far seat by the window, order mezcal.

Marco, the shy, track-suited owner, recommends the pollo. You choose the fish and, alone for a moment, drink in the worn lacquer of the room.

Y el aire se conmueve de tanta pena.

Harp silence unstrung. Four Americans (two couples), Ameroil-ers from Texas, bundle in and fluff the colonial line. Bob rates the décor a three. 'Oh come on Bob, it'll be yummy'.

Alabama errands, Dior joke shops. Jimmy Buffet in Cuba, Bruno Mars in Miami. 'You can just buy and re-sell on StubHub. Buy and re-sell'.

'Why 'bad black woman''? asks the mousse-shiny wife. 'Yeah, why was she bad'? echoes Bob. 'You know, I'd like a bad black woman, but I don't see her on the menu'. Hysteric guffaw.

'Okay, officially, my wallet doesn't fit in my pocket, we have to spend fifty bucks here on at least one damn meal'.

They look at you, unnoticing them, tired of your own prominence and ashamed. Their faces, stretched by surgery, do not blink.

Gonzalez's 'Andarelle': Yo soy negro, sí señores. Y no niego mi color.

El ser negro no es afrenta.' I am black, yes sirs. And I do not deny my colour. Being black is no shame.

They ask you what you do, why are you eating alone. You tell them you are a government spy. 'Heard of Julian Assange?' They laugh eagerly, like you are the prize clown at a birthday party.

And the air is moved by so much pain.

From the window you see a young girl under the archway slowly bashing her head on the wall. 'Fake them to make them. That's so funny. You know, barcodes are easy. The taxi driver was Iranian. *Sure* he was'.

Rare Japanese whisky, safari kills. Virgin White: The Most Expensive Tea in the World. Two thousand dollars a cup. 'Don't tell them you're not a virgin, Janice, being white is fine. Would you eat a fox if it were served to you on a plate with a rich sauce? *Of course* you would'.

Regurgitate the plot like a failed novel. The house vino sent back for Chilean Chardonnay. 'Oh, I see, we're in some black lady's house. So, where is she?'

She stands on the mouth of a crocodile, chained to her wings under the mountain of Pichincha. Aluminium clouds kneel down to Sucre at the altar of the motherland.

Overnight, a scarf of mist folds its arms over Quagua.

Y el aire se conmueve de tanta pena.

And what have you done in doing nothing?

Nothing. I have done nothing.

And the air is moved by so much pain.

In the morning you climb the mountain, ask the summit guide about the battle of 1822. His reply is slow, as if eking something difficult out, like blood from a blister.

'The Spanish weren't taking aim, they were just shooting a volcano… And then it burst. And only then we were free.

ISTANBUL $\longrightarrow$ GAZIANTEP

'TO BE HERE WHERE YOU SHOULD BE'

for F

Guilty as privilege. To be here where you should be. But not here.
Weighing kofte bari, cemen otu behind the splint-fillings of Yeni
mosque. No words for no word from the smuggler broker. To call.
Not to call. To be left waiting on the end of the line. To uselessly
pull apart Kurdish rugs, haggling over prices as they price you up.
Money rots. Your elders are cashed out/into the unravelling bribe.
Call it what it is. Wary over Whatsapp [Delete this.........Delete].
Red blush tomatoes slip too easily down the throat. Mesopotamian
host eyes the cost of an oil truck stuttering across the Bosporus.
You are crammed around your uncle's tv watching Premier League
re-runs. Choose wisely not to celebrate, sliding in the winning goal
on Cox's beach. You turn your face into someone else. Your name
into Bangla. Send the visa a week ahead but still the flight grounds
another and again. On Büyükada, a Turkish flag severs the landing
boat. You wait, linger at water like the Marmaran sea tunnelling into
white haze. To hear no news changes nothing. Everything. A crow
shatters the window pane. Stares at its own reflection. Unable to fly.

Dilek Taşi. Place a hand on the wish column. The sweating column.
Laugh out your tears on the weeping column. Scree your hand anti-
clockwise. Cool it on a marble jar from Pergamon. If the muezzin's
voice holds until the last note, it rings for truth. But whose? One wish.
To walk freely through Imaret's gate. As if leaving were simplicity.
One footstep to another. For you to travel anywhere without so much
as a bow. Without fear of misdirection. The security guard at the door
rattles prayer beads behind his back. Another counts tourists through
the treasury chamber to a Minbar where Mary rings the dome, holds
her immaculate son on the divan's white eiderdown. That you could
walk from the Malfili of Murad aligning yourself with the blue/green
mosaics and speak your name: Allah. Jesus. That the hand of another

will carry you through the sky. The holy texts are bound by the same tiles but the Imam's translation of the ten commandments does not fit, says the guidebook. And yet all the gold in the bazaar passes beyond skin. On the diesis, a precursor asks Christ to intercede on the behalf of humanity. Hand poised, but the eyes look past you asking: why?

A blue dome's improbable fold leaves no room for error. How the light breaks through. You do not trust it you say (since no-one can be trusted). Don't tell them any names or dates. Wipe out the messages as you go. A signature innocuous as the mark of a fingernail clawing at a wall. No-one is working on Hagia's southern restoration, but the scaffold remains. It has been like this for years now, says the guide shuffling in a cast of expensively bored Russians. Place your hand in the column, ask for someone else's luck. For the garden of Constance to unlock. For the emperor's green door (güzel kapi, the Beautiful Door) to open just for you. Dilek Taşi. Place your hand on the wish column. Sweat out the mythamous of history. Laugh your tears aloud. Under Sofia, Medusa's head is caught sideways by Perseus, Poseidon [insert other names here]. The column trickles down, 100ft filled, it's said, with the tears of slaves. In the darkness you thought no one was looking, but he is here always, changeable as sky: Christ to Apollonius. In the dark, unsure, unbeliever, to pray beyond the everywhere corruptibility of it all. Because anyone should be free to walk through a door and drink in this sun, this stiff air.

for C

Town of the wounded veteran. To Gaziantep from where did you come? The same question asked each day. Are farmers burning off the pistachio fields, or is it something else? The burning of the bomb. A boy lights up the wickertip of a pomegranate and feints to throw it in your direction. Pigeons in the bulger yard at Yabinskent scatter through the street's arid cracks. Only a U-bend road past the mosque. No purpose in driving past Allah says the guard, so you don't but are still stopped at the checkpoint. Are you Kurdish? he asks. You are Kurdish. Syria? Iraq? You hand over a Turkish passport. 'Always Turkish is last', you whisper back to the bus. 'Don't worry about it, these fuckers do the same thing to me every week back in Istanbul'. 'Ahh, Turkey', confirms the guard, sending his footman for the paperwork. Silence flaps like laundry from tower blocks. The city opens out like hammered collage. The poets crawl from the bus, hand over IDs, smoke in the dust. A minaret pierces the sky through a fist of cloud and the guard's glare locks until Turgay (the Jack Nicholson of Turkish television) steps from the bus to ask what's wrong. Sudden friendship. Laughter's echo. Everything is forgotten in the singing of autographs.

Who drags the girl by the cloth of her hijab, picking bin litter for tin cans. Kurdish-Syrian, maybe twelve, what threat is she? A pink rose blushes outside your lobby door where a UN jeep leaves for Idlib to watch on with binocular kits and empty reports. What is this pull, this human weight, but cost? She wrestles loose, runs into the darkness of the street and is gone and no-one comes out. An alleyway draped with oversized Turkish flags. Nationalist celebrants stoked by the chat show. You protest against white noise static. In Syria, on the brink of war ten years ago, you remember how the taxi drivers would place a photo of Assad somewhere in the cab or else traffic fines, worse. Lose your licence or suffer the beating, which is it and where did you go? The hotel in Tartous had other names beyond The Green Lizard and on the last day you were lost inside its labyrinth. Open the door to a conference room of soldiers, a hundred, maybe more. Another kind of breakfast was going to be served there. In the dead-end darkness a mutilated bag sags in the wind. The price of the discarded, anonymous tin: human dignity. The traffic policeman lets the girl go, throws her hijab in the air and screams down a speeding car on the road.

Nizar, so quiet from the bridge. Nobody watches from the watchtower.
Night is its own law. One eye trained towards the border's gauze smoke,
another surveys a patched-up dam shelved just above the refugee camp.
Every time I want to write a poem, says Nihat, I dive into the flooded
village of my childhood. Screenshots reveal him goggled, swimming
through his old house, school. Who said suffering is optional never lived
anywhere far from their armchair. The Euphrates smothers rubble into dust.
Water rises to wash away the myth of black roses. In Nizar, refugees
are first documented then assigned a temporary tent. You cannot live here,
ringfenced, no rock to build a root. The houses from Birecik emblazoned
with bilious mist. The best hope, says Selahattin, is to end up somewhere
else. Another town or village. Families are separated by work, location.
In the pistachio fields around Gaziantep there's no such thing as a landowner
spending his profits from the sun. Chained to the wall, a dog barks.
The geese stand up and scatter, wake the overseer, asleep in his chair out
-side the windowless house. A plane echoes turbinal across distant hills.
All the land is bordered. There is always someone there to meet you.

BREMEN → HAMBURG

'Pyramid form represents hierarchies'

To exist not to exist. To exist inside the betterment of a future.

Put your hands to your ears as in Munch's Das kind und der Tod. Say something back to the almond eyes of Modersohn-Becker's Mädchenkopf.

Beckmann's Sinnenda Frau turns and looks off into the grey distance. And still this throbbing.

An EU flag irises your hair. The Schipol falls into a rising sun. Hunter valley green.

To exist, inside the jaw of a caught whale.

World
spinning, don't slip
away.

Over Bürgermeister bridge, children protest: one with a paper globe declaring KAPITALISMUS.

Child. Listen to the grown-up children who do not listen to you. They are wearing tailored suits and speak inside the static of *world-wide radio*. Android corporate on speakerphone. The sponsor for tonight wears a logo called JOKE. The replicants are laid out like stencilled furniture under heat lamps.

Child. Someone decided this is X. The exact point where the aliens will land.

Du spricht. Keine. Keins. The dayweight lump in your stomach.

You wait inside the absence of a window, count a sparrow's footprints. Malt of sleeplessness. The room cleans itself when you close the door.

Animal in a sensorial zodiac. The auditorium waits for you to speak but you cannot remember yourself beyond the functionaries of language. Two hundred hearts beat in mirror wind.

In heavy-breath silence, the culture secretary's jewellery titters. Everything gold down to the subtitles.

Because touch touches everything, moves through everything, why is it nothing touches you?

As if life meant waiting for someone else. Don't touch me.

You write a letter to Gasquet on the riverbanks of the Weser. Little more than a creak in the wind of language.

You write: your tribunes are filled with silt. Strike it out. Revision: your tributes are filled with the filthiest of secrets.

To edit yourself out. Another kind of dying. Your hair crooked in the photobook.

You drag your Hippolytean iron foot. A simple valgus. Hunnishly indecent. In the archive footage, Bovary's eyes twitch like the wings of a butterfly.

Talus. Fenêtre. Optimal storage of the eye. The beating skin of the canal. Time's colour, soured only by time.

> The children
> demand nothing,
> only a planet.

A portrait of rain weeps into fern shadows of the lake. Get up from your attic posing, shake loose the blinds.

In the Gak, Cézanne's artillery war against Impressionism. Chamomile and cow parsley in the pallet of Monet. Paint the bloodbody. The soulfall.

Between gradients of catastrophe and ignition, you blanch at posterity. Live for a speckle of sunlight on the sitter's throat.

Blanched out. The field shucked to a sinew of roots. The sniper's eye misses, in-blinks. Pull your skin over your face and then what?

The hand-me-down of public view. Headlights stare, X-raying your face. Blue diamond backdrop. A white flag in outskirt mud.

Don't go knocking on doors here. They have invented a name for your namelessness. '[T]he murderous bad breath / of some dictator / no one wants to know anymore.'

Anymore than you. Sprötze's little pepper sack. Bodies wrapped like silkworms.

PAKO graffiti. Swastika keys. Arrivals met sternly at the gates.

> As if hate
> could rival
> yourself.

The cab driver at Hamburg was an interpreter for the US army in Afghanistan. Last year they refused him entry. So his family are at home and he's pretending to be here with you, driving through the veins of the Elbe.

What echoes. What coheres. Look into the light, away from sacristy, salvation. Away from yourself to the Hanseatic city.

U-shaped burnholes outstare the Baum wall. New recruits in khaki tread planks at Landungbruken laughing at Captain San Diego, Willy Brandt. Cigarette smoke cauterises through yellowy teeth.

On pleated water you float. Defence: a pageant of confidence. Platzen for Cartier and pleasured grimaces of the Reeper(bahn).

What brought you here and through which door does your conscience leave?

Inside the hipster hotel they are selling quotes from Goethe on the lids of jam jars. Umbrellas to pay for the rain. 'Wo viel Licht ist, ist starker Schatten' Where there's a lot of light, there's a stronger shadow.

You tap-tap the ankerstock, nothing but wind. You jigger a gaff sail, nothing but stitches in the wind's mouth.

You ask yourself: what splits the world more: ideas of men, or men of ideas? Action or religion? Christopher Columbus puddling his pesto on the plate or Pope Alexander praying to the god of war?

Lepanto. Alexandra. Hamburg. Liverpool. Your losses. Your token demons nailed to the mast. Your squadrons anchored. Your race-built Galleon Bull.

And every little
ship overboard
with silence.

You sign off the Brevisma with ideas of Ascension. The bloodcake of the world sliced open. Held to the lockchain of Sklaven Ketten (kettled slaves).

You sign off the offsetted death rates with rationales of human merchandise tallies and space allocation. Just like the unfairness of Fair Rosamond. Nothing *great* about the Great Elector.

Beyond imagination, the wielding of empire. Sink inside your own mouth for a mother of pearl medicament box.

Pox on your Bredenhof, your Pollox. Brackish your Rumfass. Tyrell stares through the cracked paint of his face. Deadliness of certitude.

After the firestorm. After the dreadnought. After the patron seas of sailors.

To see the harpooned bone of the ocean. His acidifying face abhorred by the sea.

'Nimm meine Hand, und ich führe Dich zu Dir zurück.' Take my hand and let me lead you back to yourself.

So you go. Into the sinking of PH, blaming the impaired formation of time. 'Eternal beginner, new in your mistakes.'

To St Nikolau, where the steeple raises, not towards the construction of heaven, but the closing eyes of a blackened gargoyle over Reimersbrücke. Carpet ash of rooftop shells.

Every window blown out, but for your window. Lilyface white and ossified. Sidespun into practical dysfunction.

Your eye blinks inside the telescope. Leads to the where, back to yourself. As if to ask: what use are you merely cogging up the machine room engine (that is time)?

A liftshaft jolts. Memory shakes the viewfinder. You focus in on the Museum of Dungeons. A skeleton held from its head by a rope.

In the church, you light a candle and place it inside the gargoyle's mouth. Men of war: is there anything more violent than this fragility?

The echoes do not cohere. Write me an elegy beyond sacristy. Amen.

IHR LEBEN FÜR EUCH. The Elbphilharmonie singing inside and out.

> White oratorium.
> Brücke's darkness,
> a chorus.

During the Lampedusa scenes, the woman in F6 is uncomfortable, crosses her leopard skin trousers, scratches the perfection of her brow.

'With the uncleansed tear, in despair (one day despair will drive me to despair).'

'Nein, wir hätten nicht kommen sollen' replies her husband, examining the golf ball face of his watch.

Why is it every stringed instrument is plucked by a white hand? Scream inside the sea's orchestra, but only the are fish listening.

A shrimp shell echoes with salt. A lighthouse, tongue-sharp, its singing bell freezeframes the crawling cruise liner.

All elegy is a held note –

You track your footprints in snow at the Berlin Victory Monument. You have been up all night, watching Churchill's greasy finger blot the sky with fire. Boil the stars of Europe.

Groggy, you search for coffee only to find food menus. From your window, Hafen City's dredged propeller, unmoved.

You go to the Kunsthalle, extended as pro-tag. Faces of gaping blank holes stare through the human graph where the only distinguishable word is HOPEFUL.

14.40 over 560. You write it down but do not understand the equation.

It is about making choices: tick the NERVOUS box or the UNEASY box. As if choosing between statesmen and businessmen.

If someone could tell you why the card measures at 4x3 inches for seven days in February, it might all work out right.

On the map, blue is Israel. Syria red. Palestine missing. The manifesto declares protest as anti-ammunition. If red is 40%, how do you live without it?

Weaponries meaning stock prizes. NATO receipts.

'A game is their history, / unbloodied, older than ours, / They don't need historians, / henchmen…'

And so, splinter music. And so, a clock ticks above the bomb. Step this way says the businessman. I can stop you dead like a rattlesnake's eye.

You save the date. 24th June, 2045. When the financial singularity crashes. When the visor finally slips from your face. Or else this and with clearface heavies to tell you about it.

Gross capital cut-ups intended as much as stampbook fixities. How low might you go for half a kilo of speck? Car windows for 2hr limits. Mosques turning grey.

Every small consolation tradeable. Skeletons at the money counter. The bugs have their own voices and Goethe has been looking down on you, the unplucked chicken.

Your face shrinks into lines. A man who can grow numbers on his hands waits to count you at the weigh-in.

If you want to know why all this is happening ~~I don't want to know why this is happe~~ try speaking with the on-dead.

You pull away from the handshake and listen in. One ear busy with the voices you hear between radio stations.

You wheeze on a cane-backed chair, too tired to sit up or speak out, your finger on the dial of the late night local shock jock.

To talk with you, eye to iris, as if through a veneer of smoke. The glass on your mother's portrait breaks in your hand and her blood (yours) is speaking blood.

All elegy, a held note –

> father, wounded
> by language, what song
> you sing?

Speak. Speak to remember. But I don't want to remember, he replies.

The sky over Adolphplatz: enough spit to hiss rain.

On the harbour at Niederhafen, the cries of a gull strain through noise-cancelling headphones.

Silence turned up on the Domschorf. Chameleonic laughter in the Friseur salon. Yellowtipped dockposts: matches struck against the night. A city's heaving circuitboard of water.

Over the Elbe, everything wears the false simplicity of order. Woodcuts soil the trees. A faint shadow on the horizon. Fields tilled into lines.

You hover until jolted back into the weird turbulence of living.

Somebody is speaking about safety procedures. But you never voted to proceed.

BUENOS AIRES $\longrightarrow$ MONTEVIDEO $\longrightarrow$ BUENOS AIRES

'QUERIDO ES MUY BIEN AQUI'

A s if you might be full of grace only to walk among us. As if you might candle the dark.

Sky fades to blackout. A solitary candle on Salta. Pearled globelight of moon on the Avenida de Mayo. Forty four million people engulfed in a power cut. The rain lathers your ears like soap.

The Catedral Primada de Buenos Aires is lit up, as if by gold reserve. EGO VICI MUNDUM. AVE GRATIA PLENA. Tourists pose sideways at the church nave. So many photos for the immaculate.

If you were beautified once then what is this moment but the light decaying inside you?

Ya encendrum las lámparas. / En los golfos de Sombra. They have lit the lights / in the gulfs of shadow.

San Miguel stands on the head of a chained man, black hollows for eyes. Lord, you whisper: defend us with your life.

At the altar, a bearded man – handsome, ruffled and thin, no more than thirty – smells of sweat and faeces. No-one prays there.

> To separate syllables from
> blood. To repose desire.
> Just a little light
> to stop this humming.

A hole in the sky outside the Ministerio de Trabajo. A mural of rusted cogs rises to Trump's doppelgänger taptapping a keyboard.

Someone will have to wash this off. Someone will have to fix this. Not you or the security guard watching from the corner of the street.

Suspense of cranes over the Hilton from high offices on Tucumán. A family sleep under arches. The mother's eyes fizz open with each passing splash of traffic.

From high windows on Lima, you see everything microscopically. A crow snatching at the low nests.

A man outside Piedras in his overcoat laughs up to the trisyllabic gong of the cathedral on Peña. A woman walks through Guido with functionary shoes and a new bob hairdo. Another woman pearls children's knitwear on her lap and the informer asks why she doesn't speak castellano Spanish. A man fits boxes inside boxes all day, selling mate flasks. Santa María, praise him, draped in the national flag.

What is it you mean when you write 'man' or 'woman'? The babysuit, eggwhite blue, ill-fitting.

Sometimes my own skin feels too uncomfortable to wear, says Maria, over bocadillos. Sometimes people look at me with firehouses in their eyes.

Obeliskian shadow over the POLICIA vans. Blue lights on Sarmiento. Two policeman wait in a parked car licking empanada oil from the stubs of their fingers. Another day's deposit in misdeed.

The dogshit in St Elmo stains the paving, leaves a scar.

You try to say something but saliva catches with the blood in your voice. Scrape of cutlery, a reprieve.

70

What can I say to you if you ask, but do not ask for anything? Travel the root of your mouth only to unspeak.

A newborn baby pushchaired past, stares her mother down,

> as if to ask:
> what is this world
> you have made
> for me?

L ast night, the neighbour beat his wife and you did nothing. Jewellery stones scattered on the bare wooden floor. And you, with your broken Spanish, sat on the bed with arms folded, only getting up to smoke.

Pillowcase of wind, a dream's playing card. The wound of a word. The mouth speaking from its trough of blood.

You dream inside rapids. As in Páramo, you hear rain through walls, grave talk.

And yet, by morning – in a clear sky and with the power back – everything appears to have turned like a weather vane.

You pat down your pockets as if you have forgotten something. Head for the Mercado del Progreso in Caballito. Chop-chop of meat staining your apron. A butcher laughs as he cuts fat from the leg. Mallets the milanesa.

Wet rain on onionskins seethe from the Puerto Esperanza. Peperoncino heat jams the air red.

You cannot decide between the equal gesture of melons and lemons. You buy a box of mangoes, fumble between expression and expressure at the till.

Two horneros peck over the weight of sugar crumbs.

Either the neighbours will divorce or die married, you think.

A nd if they can make flames from hands, what's next? A sparrow's beak held by a keychain to keep its mouth shut. In the canvas, she places her hands together through the jail cell bars, prays from a severed neck.

Take this for your flapping tongue. There's a stepladder to the clouds. Can you hear the aviary whistling of heaven?

What was disappeared was never found in La Plata. The minister's mouth is moving but he says nothing. He just loves to eat and eat.

In Soho, when you asked the not-yet prime minister if the table were free, he said: 'no, I eat furniture'.

Minujín's recipe of Thatcher: corned beef on a meathook. Rosa Luxemburg available in pink pots. What does it matter if others protested for you?

You walk from the gallery into Puerto Madero's fog-braided arms. Rusted navy boats, sunlight ensanguines the water. Tinctured as filigree, then gone.

La Boca, gash-mouthed. The water disrobes, covers up.

Desaparecidos. Drugged up, pushed from a plane into the sea.

You confess everything, skin still humming from the rack. Deadsticks between rivulets. They call you *las locas*, the mad women.

Outside the Plaza del Mayo. DÓNDE ESTÁN, LOS CENTENARES DE BEBES NACIDOS EN CAUTIVERIO? Tell me: where is the innocence of my child?

Transparencies of fish scales. Stubbornness of the lotus. Colonia's outposts shadow the white face of your page.

You sit in the Café London, sipping your café con leche. A little more sugar. What do you care?

Was it here? Here? The military commando called those who disappeared the 'forever absent'.

To want for no other news of you (except of you). Gelman, exiled in Rome: 'Like an everyday otherworld.'

Doves fly from the Estadio Monumental over Videla's shoulder a few streets from the navy's torture centre.

Songs of Heredia
pirate on the radio.
What disappeared was
never found in La Plata.

Chassis shake and the wheels loosen underneath. Untie the horse tied from the stake beside a blank billboard. Write yourself into the big screen.

A VENDO. BANCHEROS. Dig underneath the vertebrae of border trees fanning out to the mirador of the sea. Cemetery lawns for sale and the meathouse, pegged, as if between washing lines. The sierra leans an ear, eavesdropping on the oak trees.

Sección 3 inlanded to the left. Sección 4 over La Paz and Valdense with its Ciudad Jardines and Pepsi shacks and Santanders. Spanish pesetas cover the eyes of the dead.

You head east to south along the 1, past Santa Regina's skunk fields tending a flock of sheep. She who refused Olybrius to proconsul lives in immortality, carrying her own head.

If reality is the logging of a forest, better to believe in mythos. Blink into silence. Every flame in the fire, various as an alphabet.

What is imperceptible is merely yet to form into sense. Turbines wind anti-clockwise. You sit in your house all day smirking at the television with the grills down.

Self-scioned. Short-circuited by the advertising jingo. Get up.

During the Paraguayan war you spoke in code. If the stove is open, come on in. If the chimney smokes with ash, wait for me at the ranch. If there are two candles on the window's parapet, they are watching us. If the Rotunda door is painted with a red circle, above all, do not enter.

Mirage of rain clouds. There's light parading through the blinds from the west. Won't you come in? Come in.

You enter Pocitos. Piano and panpipes at Garcías. You are tired, deserving of what you don't understand. Familia Deica's cherry notes inhaled straight from the branch. Repetir, por favor.

You order the baby lomo and the waiter shares you as the punchline with his Venezuelan server. Clear the plate but for a blood puddle of ketchup. He does not return.

You lick the seafoam from your lips and spit against the wind, asking yourself: what is the question hanging over every idea of country?

Gandhi turns away from his own statue on La Playa. Beyond him, a port, a boat and, beyond this, La Plata with its steelcut waves, its fishfeed of bones.

In India this week, a BJP minister said he would throw all immigrants out, pointing his finger to the sea. Nationalistic discord. Disjuncts.

Three angels in a dice cup fountain. One jade, the other russet, the third grey then green in the sun. The governmental motorcade passes and nods mutely to the gardener at Plaza Matriz.

You walk through Montevideo mechanically. Wind singing inside the buckles of your new shoes. You check the map for a road that has no name and name it Skin of the Abadejo.

In the Mural de los Derechos the words: Apoyo, Respeto, Carono, Abrazo. The child in your face would like to speak.

Memory pre-discriminates says the boy in the video. For three generations you heard the same note inside the same flute. The same song echoing like a conch through the seas of the Surandina.

Sky letters. Earthnotes. Agudo y fuerte. Hold your cape like a matador against the colonial bloodwhip. Perro, Zorro, Diablo. Diablito. Jellyfish amoebas behind your eyes.

If Jali falls down in the street who will pick him up? If history led you here, then what song is singing now?

Venus speaks over the harbour. A lighthouse beam catches the statue of an enslaved woman, cut at the shoulder [UNNAMED].

You tell yourself you would band-aid her arms, but then what? Then what?

All night, wind whacking the windows. In the morning, you walk through Palermo, chest pulled in, pavonine as a spring peacock.

As if with every action a forgetting. You who wants to forget, forgets.

When a young girl slides you change in the Oro Rhine, something (guilt or desire?) sugarlumps in your throat.

A portrait of Morticia gives you the middle finger on Pablo de Maria.

In the Ciudad Vieja, you look in jewellery shops at Druzy rose earrings, Tiger Eye necklaces, Aventurine Cabochons. Leave with nothing.

On the street below, a jeweller in round, red-tinted sunglasses sells pendants, hammering amethyst and copper wire.

He senses your uncertainty and takes off his glasses to reveal heavy khol-like lines. 'I have marijuana too', he says, handing you a green bag.

Buque upgrade for a view of La Boca's
wetmouth slanting in sheet rain across
a cinema screen window. $20 the price
to blur la Puerta and beyond the door:
Clase Primera Especial. Double or nothing,
you cannot just walk through. Memory
inside a photo. As if you could re-enact this.
Rain, but it's not raining. Confetti on the fan
terrace, stilled by Buenos Aires' hot breath.
You cruise slowly into a harbour of skyscrapers, navy yard roughhouses, a uni-
formity of white yachts. The ICBC building,
a smeary, greying portrait. The guard
at the gate, eyes downcast. Run aground.

Your dog takes a shit outside Hotel Presidente.
Someone else always cleans up for the State
and it's not Alsina, busted, Socratic, his hand
remonstrating with a balding, white sky. They
rake green shoots into a pile on LIBERTAD,
a cosmetic gesture to the funerary traffic
on Avenida 9 de Julio, the largest boulevard
in the world. You film your dog in a series
of selfies cascading through the park. Abilio
roll over [click], Abilio squatting for a piss
on the lower branches by the hissing fountain
[click]. Snapchat over the traffic snaking west.
You feel yourself part of the continuum going
nowhere in the coolness of a Jacaranda's quiver.

Who was it fleecing the workers' pockets but you?
Each day opens and closes like a clockwork petal.
Even the air locks everybody in. Today is another
national holiday: warm rain soaks up the workers'
protest, where you pass by tapping your wallet,
looking down at the young man who lost his father
in the cyanide mines at Valdero. What can you say
when your eyes are spreadsheets, counting out
the world in ounces of gold. 'Lo Siento' you mutter
when the Pepsico workers approach, not meaning
I feel or feel sorry, but the formality of 'Déjame
Pasar'. And you pass. Dream of a hacksaw factory.
Even Marx backed away when he saw the flags
of free capitalism. All those numberless offices.

PAN Y TRABAJO reads the sign. PAN Y TRABAJO.
When a canvas didn't sell he drank the oils.
Turn away into Pettoruti's La Plata. They call
you a foreigner but what does the word really
mean? Look away now and again. Solar's smoke
-river. Spilimbergo's louche terrace: the world
floats through rocks like memories (but whose?).
Commotional billboards blur and set the cars
honking. Tamayo's soldiers wear shells for eyes.
Your everyday uniqueness and vertical sequencing
unimpresses Lam's balloon skull; its eyes look
away from you towards a tablecloth covered in
unshakeable dust. Carry your tears in a wet sack,
worn heavy. Until the retina starts to shriek.

Lightcrawlers. Monsters in the bestiary. Games of
love or mischance. You count your casino chips
on the side of a dice. Peel away yesterday's lover
from the tattoo map of your body. What you want
to call temptation can be renamed Ambition's Grotto,
Encounters Unease. Turn Aryan devils into saints,
rise above a city counting out your bank balance.
Rattle your new coupe keys in the exhaust, ex-
hausted, wheeze through a cloud of cognac, disc
cells contracting the rotunda of your body. Morning,
your skin ruddied, reduced to buying up the sellabilities
of image. So much distance between victory and victim,
you think (how to translate this for the boardroom?)
When you die they'll cut the film from your face.

The voyeur twiddles you as if by puppet string.
In Figari's Candombe o Candombe de carnaval,
a pink-shirted man shakes open his hands to
question a gallery of masked faces in windows.
Chevron – Swastika. A General, skeletally x-rayed.
Another morning when the waffle-haired president
reminds us how we met Hitler. As you would say,
sometimes it's all just too much. How to embody
hope? Chagall painted dreams to save the world
from itself. My hands run over yours, lean in through
the remoteness of trees to fire a kiss. Because what
else is love but the world opening in your eyes, open.
Morose beauty of a horses' eye, sad but knowing.
Stay close, take cover, safe in this mirage of mist.

Today, walking in the scent of love's blood.
Tomorrow, casted in Alonso's 'Carne de Primera'.
'It's not just in Mexico, women go missing here,
you don't hear about it on the news.' A businessman smokes his cigar and the elsewhere of his eyes
suggest: I am counting you up as a number: 622
by the leg, 729 by the arm. I live out my violence,
from the entrails of a ranch, from the hanging
of a meathook. The oligarchy are Bacon-faced,
digging another anonymous grave at the roadside.
A lost child runs through doors of broken glass.
You edit yourself in and out, as Mayakovsky
advised. It's a form of self-dentistry, he said, just
to survive. A gloved hand props open your throat.

Without bread but with work. Weeks caption
the stillness of a blue table. Nothing devastates
more than a child dangling an empty spoon.
Stray bloodfleck on black-backed curtains.
Monday: volcanic as the sun. You remember
Christmas 1990, your mother serving chicken
instead of turkey. Am-Dram pretence of knives,
but she ate none. Outside the window, a swab
of musketeering soldiers on the charge raise
the sword of war. Death breathes through the cut-
glass wetness of your eyes (but for what, what?)
A child's belly, soiled, the bills yet to be paid.
Whoever paints this is the repo man at the door.
The father looks to the mother who looks at you.

To forget is to think of the Manzano, climbing
a ladder of apple harvests. Study the way light
slants through the window and it will tell you
the heat of the day. Cacti enflamed as parakeets.
You sit between two dreams and wake between
sagging bedframes. You write out bad jokes to
become headlines, entries in encyclopaedias:
if three boys are walking towards you, which one
carries the knife? Carnicero, de la Serie el Ganado
y lo perdido. Who invited you to dance here in the
butcher's ballroom, head tangoing from the hook
of your neck? Mal de amores. Don't end up like this.
In the painting, one foot points towards the morgue.
A raw breast exposed, and you, weeping in her arms.

Dressed as a security guard, the gallerist whispers
'no escriba aquí. no escriba aquí.' Twice as if it
would mean something more than censorship,
if repeated – a firebox incendiary, some kind
of willed miracle. You presume your own mistranslation and move on to the next canvas:
lookalike of your friend Juan with his dog Ezra.
Text a photo, like the Chinese couple texting
in the corner, but the guard is walking towards
you again, repeating, 'no escriba' with the face
of a shy executioner. Only at school did they
tell you to stop writing and it started you off.
'Soy un poeta. Carlos Alonso es un pintor, y un
poeta. Todo arte vive de la poesía. ¡Libertad!'

Benarres' gato doesn't mewl any last goodbyes.
She likes to eat the meatrinds you left in private.
Put a finger between her eyes and she'll bite it.
You lean into DEFENSA, a square fraying with trees
you haven't bothered to learn the names of (even
in English). On the cobble streets of San Telmo,
sometimes you preferred it when only the footsteps
spoke. How silence often gives the best speeches.
In the taxi, Camila says tomorrow will be the time
for tears and you make the awful Perón joke,
remembering Madonna at the balcony, playing
herself. The cat licks your hand and you say:
'I trust this little one more than humans'. Its good
eye flicks away from you, towards the meat.

GRANADA

'Para las Rosas'

Madame Etoile tends the climbing vines, sunlight soaks through her skin.

A pomegranate's drowsy tissue folds into the city's lookscapes. The vine shadow of a hand applauds through five o'clock wisteria.

Scent event of rose lilac and clove. Jasmine opening the air's veins.

You take a seat and wait for history's keys to jostle in the door.

> Flesh eyes of the sultan.
> An eagle with two heads.

Ibrahim asked Mohammed to make this a secure city, to provide its people with fruits. Twelve lions spout the rivers of Jerusalem through cubed teeth.

Stalagmite emblems arc lapis outside the seven levels to heaven. Truce of doves zag through an immaculate cape of blue.

Praise be to Janna al Arif. To the garden of the architect. Peace be the dove upon your shoulder.

And yet this restlessness. This making love to your own sorrow.

Voices echo through petals summoning Isabella from the tower. A black rose buds before her eyes. Soraya. Isabella. Soraya. Isabella. Soraya. Soraya. Who are you, who are you?

Rage in the Hall of the Abencerrages, parapet to courtier. Sunsting of the harem. A stone vault rises through the Court of the Myrtles.

You wear a rose garden's paradise of thorns. You ask for a cup of rain to cool the vine's heat. All the servants who have appeared at your door, appear again at your door.

To sit beside history, the most faithful of liars. As if you could never leave with anywhere else to go.

Walls meant for moonlight, florescent in halogen. Irving's room bloodshudders a ghost.

> Who are you,
> who are you?

After the king cut off the heads (of State) he awoke in the morning with a familiar idea: first banish a language, then wear its bloodsoaked clothes.

PLVS VLTRE: ultra fear. Of self / other as self. Kiln wounds. A matchstick torches your ear.

Seeds of the Nile hyacinth splay over the afternoon's sallow light. Arrowslice the sky. Goosefeather clouds.

Your eyes fade with the sunset. *Every rent, every chasm of time.* Every day the sky transcribes love's celebration of error. A city singed, hot inside its bones.

At the outer gate, a carthorse neighs past, heavy with watermelons, limes. Eye lashed into blinking and the distant twinge of a guitar string starts up the ruined palacios.

Sing the bulls' hoof rutting inside this moon. Sing through the archer's slit. Sing to protest an empire's nimbus. Of sentries, centuries, sing. Sing into the silence. Sing to speak of this, this speaking fire.

What once healed like lavender is the sobbing child you carry on your back.

Sound to soundedness. Original language of the face.

An ugly face: Felipe the Handsome curling into a snarl, looking down on you. Flush with secrecy at the breach of Viznar.

Felipe, with his list of names and addresses. Inverse of a mountain's wounds.

Nada negra in the bowels of the canvas, eclipsed wings. Lorca's salavilla de estrella. Spit lickety on the cathedral wall.

You are here, but found to be gone. Come morning, inside Moratorio's Guerreros, naked, stung by pollen.

You dip inside a rock's silhouette. Alight in constellations of sky. Ease into the misted vega.

Who are you,

who are you?

Flesh eyes of the sultan.

An eagle with two heads.

Under the Darro, Lorca's rose-sheared clouds rumble under the Fuente las Batallas.

No time to write down the last letter in your mouth – ~~Amor~~.

Olive groves zither and shrill all the way to Vaqueros and the lost childhood of your house. The plain tilts. Riverine breath held by the Nevada.

All that is left are bottles of colonial sherry, unpaid dowries.

As if you could cool your breath in the lion's fountain. As if this evening air were your voice, folded too soon in the licked envelope of an hour.

She only asked for water to put out the fire in her eyes. But the king quickly took from his horse and slapped the young girl sideways.

Pocket rose of the Manola in a torn shirt. Franco's face smiling in darkling mirrors.

You rest on a cloud's shoulders. You break up the land to separate yourself.

NOTES AND QUOTATIONS FROM THE TEXTS

It is the intention of the author that not all spoken phrases in other languages will be translated from each section. The following notes and references are provided to assist in the reading of the these texts.

Cox's Bazar
The quotes from poems are from poets Ro Mehrooz and Zaki Ovais included in *I am a Rohingya* (Arc, 2019).
Other quotes are anonymised.
'Ze zaga añra félai ay zaígoí' translates from Rohingya as 'places we never leave'.

Dhaka → Chittagong
'Give charity from what God has given you… Should we feed the person whom God, if He wished, could feed?' This line has been taken from the Q'ran, 36:47.
'From the windows of / this / room, I sit helpless, / waiting, / silent— sister'. From Tarfia Faizullah's 'Aubade Ending with the Death of a Mosquito', published in *Seam* (2014), Southern Illinois Press.

Mexico City → Puebla → Mexico City
'Male and female slaves to be sold in the market.' is a translation from Bernal Diaz del Castillo's *The Conquest of New Spain*, originally published in 1632. Bernal was one of Cortés original army of men who invaded Mexico.
Various Spanish phrases are included in this text, including the following basic translations by the author:
- Mala Madre – Sick mother
- Pero cuando, pero / perdido – but how, but lost.
- No / jeres ir – don't let go.
- tu hermana es bonita como tu madre / Tu madre / está cansada hoy
- your sister is pretty like your mother / your mother / is tired today
'no araña o cobra, lo Innominable' (neither spider nor cobra, / the Unnameable), from Octavio Paz's 'Near Cape Comorin', published in *The Collected Poems of Octavio Paz (1957-1987), edited and translated by Eliot Weinberger.*

QUITO → ESMERALDAS → QUITO
Carmen Gonzalez's, 'Caramba' and 'Andarele' are tracks from *Caramba*, published in 2000 by Network Medien GmbH in Frankfurt. *'La razon yo / me pregunto / En donde esta la conciencia / la conciencia de esta mundo.* Where is the reason / I question / Where is conscience / the conscience of the world? is from 'Caramba'
'Yo soy negro, sí señores. Y no niego mi color. El ser negro no es afrenta.' I am black, yes sirs. And I do not deny my colour. Being black is no shame is from 'Andarelle'.
Margarita Laso's 'Tarde o temprano' is a track from the album *Vivir en Este Carpuela* published by Gallito Verde in 2001.
'Nada me ha quedado de ese tiempo en que me amabas' (Nothing has remained from the time you loved me) and 'Y el aire se conmueve de tanta pena' (And the air is moved by so much pain) are both quotes found in the Mala Negra restaurant, where Ecuadorian poets and musicians used to drink, perform and recite. The former is a song written titled 'Negra Mala' by Sergio Mejìa, the latter a lyric from an Ecuadorian popularised and sung by
María Isabel Carlota Jaramillo titled 'Guitarra vieja' (old guitar).

ISTANBUL → GAZIANTEP
The early section of this text is dedicated to a Rohingya poet denied the chance of education in Turkey despite having a scholarship to study there. The opening movements of the second section are for a Kurdish poet living in Turkey.

BREMEN → HAMBURG
All quotes are from *A History of Clouds* by Hans Magnus Enzensberger, translated by Martin Chalmers and Esther Kinsky, Seagull Books, 2018.
Further quotes are from Goethe, from the play *Götz von Berlichingen*, Act I (1773) and from Ingeborg Bachmann's 'No Delicacies', both translated by the author.

BUENOS AIRES → MONTEVIDEO → BUENOS AIRES
'Ya encendrum las lámparas. / En los golfos de Sombra' from Octavio

Paz, 'Pilares' ('They have lit the lights. / In the gulfs of shadow'). Published in *The Poems of Octavio Paz*, edited and translated by Eliot Weinberger, New Directions Press, 2012.

'Like an everyday otherworld.' is a line by Juan Gelman, from 'Rome. 6-22-80', from *Under Foreign Rain* (Footnotes of Defeat), published in *Selected Poems: Unthinkable Tendancies*, edited and translated by Joan Lindgren, University of California Press, 1997.

GRANADA
Federico García Lorca's quotes are from *De Primer Romancero Gitano, 1924-1927* (The Gypsy Ballads, 1924-1927), published in 1997 by Penguin in Selected Poems and translated by Will Kirkland.

TITLES OF PAINTED COLLAGES:
'Protect Names & Faces, Yes?' (Cox's Bazar)
'Life Raft Awaiting' (Dhaka → Chittagong)
'Hermana in the web' (Mexico City → Puebla → Mexico City)
'Injustos' (Quito → Esmeraldas → Quito)
'To be here where you should be' (Istanbul → Gaziantep)
'Pyramid form represents hierarchies' (Bremen → Hamburg)
'Querido Es muy bien aqui' (Buenos Aires → Montevideo → Buenos Aires)
'Para las Rosas' (Granada)

ACKNOWLEDGEMENTS

The author would like to acknowledge that all of the work published here was completed after invitations to attend poetry and literature related events in each country. No section was written during a trip that was not work-related.

Thank you to Friendship NGO in Bangladesh, to Shehzar Doja and to all the Rohingya poets who participated in the workshops in Cox's Bazar refugee camps. To the Circulo team for the invitation to Mexico City and the Luna de Locos festival in Pereira, Colombia. To Michael Augustin for the invitation to attend 'Poetry on the Road' in Bremen, Germany. To Juan and Camila for recommending me to the Buenos Aires International Poetry Festival, Argentina. Fernando Valverde and Nieves García Prados for their invitation to attend the Granada International Poetry Festival in Spain. To Santiago Grijalva and Xavier Oquendo Troncoso in Quito, Ecuador and Gökçenur Çelebioğlu in Istanbul, Turkey.

Earlier drafts of these texts were published in *Poetry Review*, Poetry London, *The New England Review, Edge Hill Poetry and Poetics Research Journal* (Volumes 1 & 2) and on www.forfatternesklimaaksjon.no (the issue on climate change).

Thanks to Christopher Routledge for taking photos of the original artworks. Additional thanks to Forrest Gander, Christopher Madden and Sandeep Parmar for their readings of earlier drafts. And to María Agustina Pardini for looking at the 'Buenos Aires → Montevideo→ Buenos Aires' section of this book.

James Byrne is a poet, editor and translator. His most recent poetry collections are *The Caprices* (Arc, 2019), *Everything Broken Up Dances* (Tupelo, 2015) and *White Coins* (Arc Publications, 2015). Other publications include *Blood / Sugar* (Arc, 2009), *WITHDRAWALS, Soapboxes* (both KFS, 2019 and 2014) and *Myths of the Savage Tribe* (a co-authored text with Sandeep Parmar, Oystercatcher, 2014).

Byrne received an MFA in Poetry from New York University, where he was given a Stein Fellowship ('Extraordinary International Scholar'). He was the Poet in Residence at Clare Hall, University of Cambridge. He currently lives near Liverpool where he is a Reader in Creative Writing at Edge Hill University.

Byrne is renowned for his commitment to international poetries and poetics. He is the International Editor for Arc Publications and was editor of *The Wolf*, which he co-founded, from 2002-2017. In 2012, with ko ko thett, Byrne co-edited *Bones Will Crow*, the first anthology of contemporary Burmese poetry to be published in English (Arc, 2012). In 2017, with Robert Sheppard, he edited *Atlantic Drift*, a book of transatlantic poetry and poetics (Arc, EHUP). In 2019, he co-edited, with Shehzar Doja, *I am a Rohingya*, the first anthology of Rohingya poetry in English. Byrne's poems have been translated into several languages and his *Poemas Escogidos* (Selected Poems) was published in Spanish in 2019 by Buenos Aires Poetry (translated by Katherine M. Hedeen and Víctor Rodríguez Núñez).

John Kinsella has written that "James Byrne is a phenomenon and *Blood/Sugar* is astonishing… He is a complete original." Ishion Hutchinson wrote of *White Coins*: "this is language charged with a tough, sensual contraflow music, vividly alive to inquiry and witness […] an astonishing work, one where virtù and gravitas are in concord with a hermetic passion, one fiercely and beautifully saying the unsayable."